Guinea Fowl, Backyard Poultry

Keeping Guinea Fowl

A Beginner's Guide to Breeding
and Keeping Guinea Fowl

herein. Any perceived slights to any specific person(s) or organizations are purely unintentional.

We have no control over the nature, content and availability of the web sites listed in this book. The inclusion of any web site links does not necessarily imply a recommendation or endorse the views expressed within them. Peter Franks takes no responsibility for, and will not be liable for, the websites being temporarily unavailable or being removed from the internet. The accuracy and completeness of information provided herein and opinions stated herein are not guaranteed or warranted to produce any particular results, and the advice and strategies, contain herein may not be suitable for every individual. The author shall not be liable for any loss incurred as a consequence of the use and application, directly or indirectly, of any information presented in this work. This publication is designed to provide information in regards to the subject matter covered.

Foreword

Guinea fowl are a type of backyard poultry that, though native to Africa, are becoming increasingly popular with poultry farmers all over the world. These birds are incredibly entertaining to keep as pets and they provide a number of practical benefits as well. Whether you are thinking about keeping guinea fowl as a means of pest control on your farm or you want to raise them for food, this book is a great place to start.

Within the pages of this book you will find a wealth of information about guinea fowl as pets as well as tips for raising them and keeping them healthy. By the time you finish this book you will be equipped to decide whether or not these birds are the right choice for you and, if they are, you will be well on your way in preparing to keep them for yourself and your family.

Acknowledgements

I would like to extend my sincerest thanks to my friends and family for their patient support throughout the process of writing this book.

Special thanks to my husband who always has been and always will be my rock.

Table of Contents

Chapter One: Introduction

Also known as guinea hens or backyard poultry, guinea fowl are a family of birds native to Africa. These birds are similar in appearance to pheasants with different species exhibiting different colors and patterns of plumage. Though guinea fowl are wild animals, they have also been domesticated for use as pest controllers in rural areas and as a source of food for humans - they can be used in the same way as chickens in many recipes but guinea fowl meat is said to be more flavorful.

Chapter One: Introduction

Guinea fowl farming is increasing in popularity in the United States and other countries outside of Africa. Many farmers value these birds for their ability to control insect pests such as ticks, cockroaches, termites, and grubs. In addition to helping to control insect pests, guinea fowl actually make very entertaining pets – they can be quite active and they often keep up a chorus of clicks, whistles, and chirps as they go about their business.

If you have ever considered keeping guinea fowl – whether for pest control or to raise for food – this book is a great place to start. Written in a clear and easy-to-read fashion, this book is designed to give you an informative introduction to guinea fowl and their care so you can decide whether or not these animals are a good choice for you. Only once you have learned everything you can about guinea fowl should you decide whether or not to keep them. Hopefully, in reading this book, you will find the answers to your questions and enough practical information about keeping guinea fowl that this decision becomes easy.

Useful Terms to Know

APA – American Poultry Association, the organization in charge of setting the breeding standards for poultry in the United States

Beak – the hard, pointed protrusion in the center of the guinea fowl's face; composes the bird's mouth and nose

Broiler – a young (less than 12 weeks) bird bred specifically for its meat; also called a fryer

Brood – referring to the care of baby keets; also a name for a group of keets

Clutch – the name for a group of eggs laid in one cycle

Crest – a puffy grouping of feathers on top of the head

Cock – an adult male guinea fowl

Coop – a building or structure used to house poultry; typically includes several roosts and nesting boxes used for egg laying

Cull – to remove a bird from the flock due to age, productivity, or health issues

Down – the soft, fur-like feathers that covers baby keets; may also be found on certain parts of adult birds such as under the wings

Flock – a group of poultry

Free Range – referring to birds that are allowed to roam freely in a pasture or yard

Guinea Cockerel – a male guinea fowl under one year old

Guinea Pellet – a female guinea fowl under one year of age

Hen – an adult female guinea fowl

Incubate – the process of establishing and then maintaining ideal hatching conditions for eggs; typically involves heat

Incubation Period – the period of time during which the embryo develops inside a fertile egg

Keet – a newly hatched guinea fowl

Molt – the process during which a bird sheds most of its primary feathers and then regrows them

Nesting Box – an enclosed space provided for hens where they can lay their eggs

Plumage – the feathers on a bird

Poultry – referring to birds that are raised for eggs, meat, or as pets

Roost – an elevated area where the bird can perch

Wattle – a flap of skin under the chin of a bird

Wing Clipping – a procedure during which the primary wing feathers of a bird are cut to prevent flight

Yolk – the round, yellow part of the egg; contains the genetic material of the female and male; provides nutrients for the developing embryo

Yolk Sac – a membrane surrounding the yolk of an incubating egg

Zoning – laws restricting or regulating the use of private or public land for certain purposes (such as raising poultry)

Chapter Two: Understanding Guinea Fowl

Owning guinea fowl, whether you are keeping them for food or as pets, is not something that you should enter into lightly. Like all living things, guinea fowl require a certain degree of care and unless you understand the basic needs of these animals you will not be equipped to provide the care they need. In this chapter you will learn the basics about guinea fowl so you can start to make an educated decision regarding whether or not they are the right pet for you and for your family.

1.) *What Are Guinea Fowl?*

As you may already know, the name guinea fowl is given to a family of birds native to Africa. These birds belong to the order Galliformes and the subfamily Numididae. Within this subfamily there are four different genera and a variety of different species. <u>The four genera of guinea fowl are listed below</u>:

Genus *Numida*

Genus *Agelastes*

Genus *Guttera*

Genus *Acryillium*

There are six main species of guinea fowl divided among these four genera and there are several subspecies and color variants in addition to these species. Though all of these species can be kept as pets or raised for food, certain species are more popular for this purpose than are others. The most frequently domesticated guinea fowl is the species *Numida meleagris*, the helmeted guinea fowl. You will receive more specific information about each of the guinea fowl species later in this chapter.

2.) Facts About Guinea Fowl

Guinea fowl belong to the same taxonomical order as chickens, turkey, pheasant and other gamebirds and landfowl. Sometimes referred to as "backyard poultry," guinea fowl are a type of ground-nesting bird that feeds primarily on seeds and insects. In their native habitat, guinea fowl are widely distributed throughout sub-Saharan Africa, though certain species are more localized. The plumed guinea fowl (*Guttera plumifera*), for example, is primarily concentrated in west-central Africa while the vulterine guinea fowl (*Acryllium vulturinum*) can be found mostly in north-east Africa.

For the most part, guinea fowl can be found in open habitats such as semi-desert or savannah lands. Some species, like the black guinea fowl (*Agelastes niger*) tend to inhabit forests. The helmeted guinea fowl has been introduced into a number of countries outside its native habitat – including the West Indies, India, and the United States – where it is raised for food. Some countries consume guinea fowl as a regular part of their diet while others, such as Northern and Central Europe, reserve it for special occasions such as Christmas as an alternative to turkey.

Though the details vary from one species to another, guinea fowl are large, dark-feathered birds often displaying a crest on the head. The plumage of most guinea fowl species is black or dark grey, densely covered with small white spots. When it comes to sexing guinea fowl, it is not as easy to differentiate between the sexes as it is with chickens and other poultry. Males tend to have larger helmets and wattles than females at maturity, though the size difference may be negligible. The only other difference is in the calls these birds make – males use a one-note cry while females use a two-note cry.

Domesticated guinea fowl exhibit a variety of plumage patterns, even within the same species. The natural color of the helmeted guinea fowl is referred to as "pearl" – other color variations that have been selectively bred include slate, purple, chocolate, lavender, coral blue, pewter, bronze, blonde, and pied. The size of guinea fowl may also vary from one species to another. For the most part, however, these birds grow to be about 21 to 23 inches (53 to 58cm) tall and weigh about 2.8 lbs. (1.3 kg).

Guinea fowl are very social birds so they are generally kept in small groups, called flocks. When kept singly or in groups that are too small, these birds tend to languish. Guinea fowl are monogamous which means that once they choose a mate, they stay with that mate for life. The average clutch size for guinea fowl is 6 to 12 eggs and they have an incubation period between 26 and 28 days. Though guinea fowl keets (babies) are sensitive to dampness, if they live to six weeks they are some of the hardiest land fowl you will ever come across.

Summary of Guinea Fowl Facts

Taxonomy: order Galliformes, subfamily Numididae

Number of Species: six main species, several subspecies and color variants

Habitat: sub-Saharan Africa, some more localized to certain areas or habitats

Domestication: helmeted guinea fowl most popular domesticated species

Purposes: pest control (insects), food source for humans, security against birds of prey, pets

Appearance: large, ground-nesting fowl; larger and heavier than chickens

Plumage: black or dark grey, densely covered with small white spots

Color Variants: pearl, slate, purple, chocolate, lavender, coral blue, pewter, bronze, blonde, and pied

Sexing: males tend to have larger helmets and wattles at maturity; males make one-note call, females two-note call

Size: 21 to 23 inches (53 to 58cm) tall

Weight: about 2.8 lbs. (1.3 kg)

3.) *History of Guinea Fowl as Pets*

The exact origins of guinea fowl are largely unknown, but these birds have been domesticated and raised by humans for food for hundreds, even thousands of years. Guinea fowl are native to Africa and archaeologists have uncovered evidence that guinea fowl were kept in ancient Egypt as far back as 4,000 years ago. There is also evidence to suggest that the meat and eggs of guinea fowl were consumed as a delicacy in ancient Rome.

While guinea fowl have likely been used as a food source in their native land of Africa for thousands of years, they were not introduced in the Americas until the 1500's. Shortly after the arrival of Christopher Columbus, Spanish explorers brought guinea fowl to the new world. In the decades that followed, guinea fowl have been subject to domestication and selective breeding to develop a number of new color varieties.

4.) *Types of Guinea Fowl*

The name Guinea fowl is given to a group of poultry species belonging to the order Galliformes. Within this order there are many different species, some of which have been domesticated. Though the helmeted guinea fowl is the most popular species for domestication, other species can be raised for agricultural or culinary purposes.

In this section you will find specific information about some of the most common species of guinea fowl including the following species:

- Helmeted Guinea Fowl (*Numida meleagris*)
- White-Breasted Guinea Fowl (*Agelastes meleagrides*)
- Black Guinea Fowl (*Agelastes niger*)
- Plumed Guinea Fowl (*Guttera plumifera*)
- Crested Guinea Fowl (*Guttera pucherani*)
- Vulturine Guinea Fowl (*Acryllium vulturinum*)

Helmeted Guinea Fowl (*Numida meleagris*)

This is the best known species of guinea fowl and also the most commonly kept. Helmeted guinea fowl can be found south of the Sahara in its native home of Africa, though it has also been introduced into Australia, southern France, Brazil, and the West Indies. This species has also been domesticated in India and the United States as a food source for humans.

The helmeted guinea fowl has a large, rounded body with a small head covered in blue and red patches of scaly skin, but no feathers. The plumage of this species is dark gray-black, densely covered with white spots. On top of the head is a yellow or reddish knob of bone, the helmet referred to in the species' name. Helmeted guinea fowl grow up to 21 to 23 inches (51 to 53 cm) and weigh up to 2.86 lbs. (1.3 kg). Due to selective breeding, a number of guinea fowl breeds have been proposed with varying plumage patterns and colors developed from the helmeted guinea fowl.

White-Breasted Guinea Fowl (*Agelastes meleagrides*)

The white-breasted guinea fowl is a medium-sized bird, growing up to 18 inches (45 cm) long at maturity. As suggested by the name, this species has black plumage on most of its body with a white breast. The head is small and bare, covered with scaly red skin while the beak is brown and the feet grey. It is particularly difficult to tell the differences between the sexes of this species, though females tend to be smaller.

The white-breasted guinea fowl is most closely related to the black guinea fowl and it can be found in the subtropical regions of West Africa throughout Ghana, Guinea, Sierra Leone, Liberia, and Cote d'Ivoire. Unfortunately, large-scale habitat loss has contributed toward placing this species on the IUCN Red List as "vulnerable."

Black Guinea Fowl (*Agelastes niger*)

The black guinea fowl is also medium-sized, having black plumage all over its body. The head of this species is small and bare, covered by pink scaly skin. There may also be a small crest of downy feathers on the crown and forehead as well as parts of the throat and neck. Males of this species exhibit three spurs on their legs while females have only one spur, if any at all.

In terms of sexual dimorphism, the males of the species tend to be larger than the females. The average size of the black guinea fowl is about 17 inches (42cm) in length with a weight of up to 1.5 lbs. (0.7 kg). Black guinea fowl tend to gather in small groups, travelling through the undergrowth on the primary and secondary levels of forested woodland. An interesting fact about this species is that it has been found to be resistant to certain diseases known to affect poultry including heartwater and various bacterial infections.

Plumed Guinea Fowl (*Guttera plumifera*)

The plumed guinea fowl exhibits the same general appearance as other guinea fowl, having a rounded body covered in black feathers, densely spotted with white dots. What makes this species different is the presence of a high, straight crest of black feathers on top of the head as well as a long wattle on either side of the beak.

There are two subspecies of plumed guinea fowl – the Cameroon plumed guinea fowl (G. p. plumifera) and Schubotz's plumed guinea fowl (G. p. schubotzi). Both species have a bare head covered in grey skin, though Schobotz's plumed guinea fowl often exhibits orange patches on the face and neck. The Cameroon plumed guinea fowl can be found from southern Cameroon to the Congo River Basin and in parts of Gabon and Angola. Schubotz's plumed guinea fowl lives in northern Zaire in the African Rift region.

Crested Guinea Fowl (*Guttera pucherani*)

The crested guinea fowl tends to inhabit open woodlands, forest, and forest-savannah areas in sub-Saharan Africa. This species grows up to 20 inches (50 cm) in size and weighs between 1.6 and 3.4 lbs. (0.72 to 1.54 kg) at maturity. In terms of appearance, the crested guinea fowl typically has dark plumage, densely covered in small white spots with a black crest on the top of the head. The appearance of this crest varies among subspecies with some having soft down and others curly feathers.

There are five subspecies of crested guinea fowl, listed below:

- Malawi crested guinea fowl (*G. p. barbata*)
- Kenya crested guinea fowl (*G. p. pucherani*)
- Sclater's crested guinea flow (*G. p. sclateri*)
- Lindi crested guinea fowl (*G. p. verrueauxi*)
- East South African guinea fowl (*G. p. edourdi*)

Vulturine Guinea Fowl (*Acryllium vulturinum*)

This species of guinea fowl is the largest species, growing up to 24 to 28 inches (61 to 71 cm) at maturity. These birds tend to inhabit the forested regions of Central Africa and they are only distantly related to the other species of guinea fowl – their closest relative is the white breasted guinea fowl (*Agelastes meleagrides*).

Vulterine guinea fowl exhibit a similar body shape to most guinea fowl, having a rounded body and a small, featherless head. The wings, neck, legs, and tail of this species are longer than other guinea fowl, however. This species has a blue face, black neck, and a long cape of blue and white glossy hackles over black plumage on the back and blue on the breast. Vulterine guinea fowl are a gregarious species, typically living in groups of 25. During breeding season, this species lays clutches of only 4 to 8 eggs, hiding them in the grass.

5.) The Roles of Guinea Fowl

There are many reasons why you might consider keeping guinea fowl. Not only are these birds a great source of food for humans, but they can also play a practical role at home or on the farm. These birds eat a number of insect pests and they can even help to protect your other poultry from large birds of prey. <u>In this section you will receive an overview of the different roles or purposes guinea fowl may serve including</u>:

- Pest control
- Deterring poultry predators
- Source of food
- Entertaining pets

a.) Pest Control

Guinea fowl are known to consume a large number and a large variety of insects on any given day. These birds are not picky when it comes to the type of insects they eat which means that they are great for controlling insect pests. Not only will guinea fowl eat things like grubs, ants, grasshoppers, flies and other common insects but they will also eat insect pests such as wasps and deer ticks that may carry Lyme disease.

b.) Deterring Poultry Predators

While guinea fowl are not necessarily aggressive birds, they have several characteristics which make them great deterrents for common poultry predators. The noise these birds make is often enough to deter rodents that might steal eggs and guinea fowl are not afraid to kill a snake that sneaks into the hen house. Guinea fowl have also been known to serve in the same capacity as guard dogs – they might not attack an intruder, but they will certainly make enough noise to alert you to the presence of a threat. The noise these birds make may also help to deter large birds of prey that could target smaller poultry.

c.) Source of Food

Helmeted guinea fowl are the species most commonly raised for food, though many species of guinea fowl are regularly consumed in Africa, their native land. Compared to chicken, guinea fowl meat is somewhat dryer but it is also leaner and has a little bit more protein. Guinea fowl meat has approximately half the fat content of chicken and fewer calories. Additionally, guinea fowl eggs are richer than chicken eggs which makes them a delicacy.

d.) Entertaining Pets

Guinea fowl are naturally curious birds and they make very interesting pets with their penchant for exploration and noise-making. The noise these birds tend to make does pose a challenge, however, if you have close neighbors.

Chapter Three: What to Know Before You Buy

Now that you know the basics about guinea fowl, you may be ready to learn some of the specifics regarding their care. Before you go out and buy a handful of guinea fowl keets, you need to make sure you are prepared to care for them – this includes learning the practical aspects of keeping guinea fowl. In this chapter you will learn about licensing requirements for guinea fowl and you will receive answers to your questions regarding how many to keep, whether they can be kept with other poultry, and the pros and cons of guinea fowl as pets.

1.) Do You Need a License?

Owning guinea fowl is not the same as owning a traditional pet like a cat or dog. For one thing, guinea fowl must be kept outside and they generally require a great deal more space than either a cat or dog would. Because guinea fowl must be kept outside, guinea fowl owners are subject to zoning restrictions and regulations which determine what animals can and cannot legally be kept in certain regions. These zoning requirements vary from one region to the next, so you will need to do a little bit of research to determine whether or not you can keep guinea fowl in your area. Below you will find general information regarding the legality of keeping guinea fowl in both the U.S. and the U.K.

a.) Licensing in the U.S.

There are no federal laws regulating the keeping of guinea fowl in the United States – legislation and zoning restrictions are regulated at the state level. In order to determine whether or not you require a permit or license to keep guinea fowl in your area, you will need to check with your state's fish and wildlife service. Some states, like

Florida, consider guinea fowl a type of domesticated poultry so no permit is required to keep them.

Keep in mind that just because it is legal to keep guinea fowl in your state (with or without a license) you are still subject to zoning restrictions. Check with your local council to see whether there are any zoning restrictions against keeping guinea fowl in your area. Even if you are allowed to keep guinea fowl, there may be certain requirements for how much land you can dedicate to their use as well as requirements for fencing.

b.) Licensing in the U.K.

In the U.K. there are various laws protecting wild birds, but guinea fowl are considered a type of poultry and are not covered by laws restricting the capture and keeping of wild birds. You will, however, be subject to complying with legislation regarding the care and keeping of poultry species as set forth by the government. In order to keep guinea fowl, you must register your flock with the Department for Environment, Food and Rural Affairs (Defra) via the Great Britain (GB) Poultry Register.

You will only be required to register your flock if you own or keep more than 50 birds on your property, even if it is only for part of the year. Though individuals keeping fewer than 50 birds are not legally required to register their flock, they are encouraged to do so. This requirement exists for the purpose of controlling disease outbreak by targeting resources in the areas where they are most needed. Other legislation that may apply to you includes the need for an animal movement license (AML) if you plan to import guinea fowl into or out of the country.

2.) How Many Should You Buy?

Guinea fowl are social animals by nature and should be kept in small groups – guinea fowl that are kept individually or in pairs typically do not do well. For the most part, you do not need to keep guinea fowl in large groups – about one dozen is a good size for a guinea fowl flock. The more guinea fowl you keep, the more noise and mess they will make. Only if you have a great deal of space to devote to free-ranging guinea fowl should you keep a flock of twelve or more.

If you have limited space, a total of six guinea fowl will be adequate as long as you only have one male in the group. In order to keep more than one male in a group of guinea fowl you need to have plenty of space so the two do not feel threatened by each other. You should expect some territorial or aggressive behavior, but as long as you have a large area for your guinea fowl there shouldn't be too much of a problem.

3.) Can Guinea Fowl Be Kept with Other Poultry?

Guinea fowl need to be kept in fairly large groups in order to be happy and healthy, but those groups need not be entirely composed of guinea fowl. For the most part, guinea fowl get along well with other poultry species such as chickens. In fact, guinea fowl that are raised with chickens tend to be tamer than those that are not.

There are several factors to keep in mind, however, when keeping guinea fowl with other poultry. If you keep your guinea fowl with male chickens, you should expect the males of both species to fight a little bit. If, however, you keep guinea fowl with hens, you may not have a problem. In addition to problems between males of the species, you also have to worry about the transmission of disease. Guinea fowl can catch diseases carried by chickens and the disease tends to be more serious in guinea fowl. It is also possible for guinea fowl to cross-breed with other species, though it does not occur frequently and the offspring are often sterile.

4.) Pros and Cons of Guinea Fowl

As is true with any type of pet, guinea fowl have both pros and cons as pets. Before you decide whether or not to keep guinea fowl, you would be wise to learn both their advantages and disadvantages so you can make an informed decision. In this section you will learn both the pros and cons of keeping guinea fowl.

Pros for Guinea Fowl

- Fairly low-maintenance pets – can be penned or allowed to roam free with only nighttime shelter
- Very hardy fowl, can survive a variety of conditions (except for snow)
- Meat is leaner and more flavorful than chicken; also higher in protein and lower in fat
- Can serve as pest controllers; they eat wasps, ticks, grubs, flies and other insect pests
- May be kept with other types of poultry, if necessary

Cons for Guinea Fowl

- Can be very noisy as pets; not recommended if you have close neighbors

- Hens lay eggs only seasonally and the keets are fairly delicate until 6 weeks of age
- Generally do not do well with confinement; prefer to be free-range, need a great deal of space
- May be subject to licensing or zoning restrictions in certain areas
- Unwanted breeding may occur – guinea fowl nest in the grass, not in nesting boxes so unexpected breeding is likely to occur

Chapter Four: Purchasing Guinea Fowl

If you have decided that guinea fowl are, indeed, the right pet for you, then your next step is to buy them! Do not just go out and buy the first guinea fowl you can find – it is important to do your research and to buy from an experienced breeder to ensure that the guinea fowl you bring home are in good health. In this chapter you will learn where to buy guinea fowl and how to pick out birds that appear to be in good health.

1.) Where to Buy Guinea Fowl

Luckily, guinea fowl have become common enough in both the U.S. and the U.K. that you shouldn't have too much trouble finding them. As an added bonus, guinea fowl keets are fairly inexpensive as well. In this section you will receive tips for locating a guinea fowl breeder and for buying healthy keets.

a.) Buying in the U.S.

Your best bet for buying guinea fowl keets in the U.S. is to find a guinea fowl farmer in your area. If the farmer doesn't sell guinea fowl himself, he will at least be able to give you some ideas for where to look. Another place to find guinea fowl keets is at state fairs and agricultural shows. Even if you do not find any keets for sale, you will have an opportunity to connect with guinea fowl keepers from all over the region from whom you may be able to buy keets. Finally, you can look online for guinea fowl breeders in your area. The Guinea Fowl Breeders Association (GFBA) is a great place to start.

U.S. Guinea Fowl Breeders:

Guinea Fowl Breeders Association Breeders List.

<http://www.guineafowl.com/GeneralStore/breeders.html>

Guinea Fowl Keets, eFowl.com.
<http://www.efowl.com/Guinea_Fowl_Breeds_for_Sale_s/5 8.htm>

Ralph Winter Guinea Farm.
<http://www.guineafarm.com/availability/>

Guinea Fowl International Association Breeders List.

<http://guineafowl.international/breeders/>

b.) Buying in the U.K.

Buying guinea fowl in the U.K. is not remarkably different from buying in the U.S. You may have luck finding a local guinea fowl farmer or breeder in your area from whom you can buy or, at the very least, receive a recommendation for a breeder. You can also view breeders lists from the national Guinea Fowl club as well as the Guinea Fowl International Association. Do not forget about farm shows in your area – these are a great way to get connected with local farmers or breeders from whom you may be able to buy keets.

U.K. Guinea Fowl Breeders:

UK Guinea Fowl.

<http://ukguineafowl.co.uk/guinea-fowl/>

Guinea Fowl UK.

<http://www.guinea-fowl.co.uk/13-furtherinfo.html>

Guinea Fowl International Association Breeders List.

<http://guineafowl.international/breeders/>

Buttle Farm, Wilkshire.
<http://www.buttlefarm.co.uk/guinea-fowl>

2.) How to Select Healthy Guinea Fowl

Once you finally make the decision and are ready to buy your guinea fowl, the worst thing you can do is to rush the purchase. If you are not careful about who you buy your keets from, or if you do not take the time to check the keets before you bring them home, you could end up with unhealthy birds that will either die shortly after you bring them home or spread disease to your other poultry. On the following page you will receive a list of tips for evaluating the health of guinea fowl keets so you can be sure the ones you bring home are in good health.

Tips for choosing healthy guinea keets:

- Speak to the breeder or farmer before you visit the farm – ask questions about his breeding practices as well as the way he raises his keets.

- If you are not convinced that the breeder is knowledgeable and experienced, do not buy from him – not only may the keets be unhealthy, but they may also have been bred from less-than-quality stock.

- Take a tour of the breeding facilities – it should be relatively clean and kept in good order. Guinea fowl tend to make a mess so you should not expect the place to be spotless, but there should be evidence of daily cleaning – no accumulated feces or dirty bedding.

- Observe the keets to look for signs of healthy activity – if the keets appear to be lethargic or sleeping during the day, they may not be in good health.

- If possible, pick up a few of the keets one at a time to examine them for signs of illness.

- Check the eyes, nose and beak of the keets for signs of redness or discharge – the keets should be relatively clean with no obvious signs of illness.

- See how the keets react to your presence – guinea fowl are naturally curious birds so if the keets show no interest in your presence and remain lethargic, they may not be healthy.

- Check to make sure the keets are not missing large patches of feathers – they will not have developed their primary feathers yet, but their downy feathers shouldn't be patchy.

- Examine the keets' feet and legs for any raised scales – this could be a sign of guinea fowl feather mites.

- If possible, watch the guinea fowl keets being fed – healthy birds will exhibit a healthy appetite.

If, after performing all of these checks, you believe the keets are in good health you should feel free to buy them. If you have any doubts, do not risk it – try another breeder.

Chapter Five: Caring for Guinea Fowl

Now that you have learned about the practical aspects of planning for and buying guinea fowl, you are ready to learn the basics about their care. Keeping guinea fowl involves more than simply letting your birds run loose in your backyard to fend for themselves. If you want to keep your guinea fowl healthy you will need to give them a clean habitat in which to live and feed them a healthy diet. In this chapter you will learn about guinea fowl habitat and nutritional requirements as well as tips for performing necessary procedures like wing clipping.

1.) Habitat Requirements

If you have ever owned chickens, you may be tempted to think that keeping guinea fowl will be the same or, at the very least, similar. In reality, guinea fowl are incredibly different from chickens in regard to their care and habitat needs. Not only are guinea fowl less likely to become tame, but they are also much more active and require a great deal of space in their habitat. In this section you will learn the basics about creating the ideal habitat for your guinea fowl.

a.) Keeping Free-Range Guinea Fowl

The first thing you need to learn about guinea fowl is that they do not like to be cooped up. Whereas you might keep chickens and geese in an enclosed area with a chicken coop to roost in at night, guinea fowl prefer to be free range. The rule of thumb to remember when planning your guinea fowl habitat is that it can never be too large. Your best bet is to give your guinea fowl free range in a large, open area during the day and to keep them in a sheltered area at night, if possible.

If you keep your guinea fowl with other types of poultry, you may need to fence the area in which they are kept with chicken netting or another type of fencing. A large but confined area may be adequate while your guinea fowl are still young, but by the time they are full grown they will need a great deal of space to roam freely. In the wild, guinea fowl can walk as much as 6 miles (10 km) in a day. With this in mind, try to give your guinea fowl as much space as you possibly can, especially if you keep a large flock of guinea fowl together.

Some things to keep in mind if you plan to keep your guinea fowl free-range:

- Free-range guinea fowl will always tend toward being wild, you are unlikely to ever tame them.
- When guinea fowl are left to be free-range at all times, they may be more at-risk for predation.
- Free-range guinea fowl tend to lay their eggs in grassy areas, so will probably not be able to collect the eggs.
- Keets left to grow up in the wild have a high mortality rate – if you let your guinea fowl be free range, consider collecting the keets when you see them and raise them until they are large enough to fend for themselves.

b.) Providing Shelter for Guinea Fowl

Even if you allow your guinea fowl to be free-range, you should consider offering them some type of basic shelter. This shelter will give your guinea fowl a place to seek respite from rain and wind – they may also choose it as a resting place at night for protection from predators. Your guinea fowl housing does not need to be elaborate – all you need is a simple three-sided shelter or an old barn. Even a shed will do as long as it is south-facing and draft-free.

If you prefer to keep your guinea fowl penned at all times rather than letting them roam free during the day, you will need to provide at least 30 square feet per dozen guineafowl. Remember, bigger is always better when it comes to guinea fowl housing. In order to keep your guinea fowl inside the pen you will need to cover it with chicken netting or pinion the birds while they are young. Pinioning involves clipping the bird's win at the last joint (the thumb) when the keet is less than a week old. Avoid this procedure if you plan to allow your guinea fowl to roam freely so they will be able to fly away from any predators.

c.) Coop Training Guinea Fowl

If you want to let your guinea fowl roam freely but prefer to know that they are safe at night, you will need to coop train them so they recognize the coop as home. Free-ranging guinea fowl will gravitate toward flying up into the trees to sleep at night if they have not been coop trained. In order to coop train your guinea fowl you will need to build not only the coop but a pen large enough to house them comfortably for 6 to 8 weeks. It is essential that you keep your guinea fowl in the coop for this length of time so they start to recognize it as home and will come back to it at night.

While your guinea fowl are being coop trained, start to feed them at dusk. Once your guinea fowl are released to roam freely during the day, they will be more likely to return to the coop at nightfall if they know they will be fed. After 6 or 8 weeks of coop training you should begin to let your guinea fowl out of the coop during the day. It is recommended, however, that you only release about half of the flock at one time. Guinea fowl have a strong flocking instinct, so they will be more likely to return to the coop if they know the rest of their flock is there. After a few days of this you can release the entire flock at once.

d.) Keeping Guinea Fowl Safe from Predators

As you may already know, guinea fowl make great watchdogs. These birds are naturally loud to begin with and they will not hesitate to sound the alarm if a predator threatens the flock. This being the case, you may not have to worry a great deal about protecting your guinea fowl from predators because they will be very vigilant. If you live in an area where there are likely to be foxes or coyotes, however, you may need to take precautions.

One thing you might consider doing is fencing the large area in which you plan to keep your guinea fowl. If the fence is enough to keep any animals out, you may be able to clip your guinea fowl's wings so they cannot fly high enough to get out of the yard. Completely free-range guinea fowl will retreat to the higher branches of trees at night so they can stay out of reach for predators. To truly protect your guinea fowl, however, you should consider penning them at night. As long as you provide about 3 square feet of space per bird along with 7 inches of roosting space, your guinea fowl will be okay with being confined at night.

2.) Feeding Guinea Fowl

If you allow your guinea fowl to roam freely during the day
they will scavenge for food in the form of seeds and insects.
This doesn't mean that you do not need to feed them,
however – some kind of commercial poultry food is
recommended to meet your guinea fowl's nutritional needs.
In this section you will learn the basics about the nutritional
needs of guinea fowl and receive some tips for providing
them with a healthy diet.

a.) Nutritional Needs

For the most part, the nutritional needs of an adult guinea fowl will be met with daily foraging for insects, weeds, grass, and seeds. Guinea fowl will feed on a variety of insects including grasshoppers, flies, slugs, worms, caterpillars, ticks, beetles, mosquitoes and more. Greens are also a necessary part of the guinea fowls diet because it helps to aid with healthy digestion. Free-ranging guinea fowl will eat grass, weeds, and dandelion greens to meet this nutritional need.

b.) Feeding Recommendations

If you keep your guinea fowl penned, or if you want to supplement their foraging diet, you will need to feed them a commercial poultry diet. It is important to note that guinea fowl require a higher percentage of protein in their diet than do chickens. Thus, if you plan to use chicken feed for your guinea fowl, make sure it is the formula designed for laying hens because it will have a higher protein content than a standard poultry diet.

When your keets are growing, they will need a diet that contains between 24% and 26% protein for the first few weeks. Once the keets are 5 weeks old you can reduce the protein content to about 18% to 20% for the next few weeks. After the keets are 8 weeks old you can feed them standard formula which generally contains about 16% protein. It is important to note that guinea fowl should not be fed pelleted foods – they should only be given mash or crumbles.

In addition to this commercial diet, you should also offer your guinea fowl fresh greens. Leafy alfalfa is a great option for guinea fowl, though they will primarily focus on the leaves. Just make sure that you remove any leftovers after a few hours in order to avoid mold that could make your guinea fowl sick. If your guinea fowl are free-range, you may not need to offer them alfalfa but you can give them an occasional treat consisting of sorghum, millet, or wheat. Whole or cracked grains are the best, guinea fowl will typically ignore large-kernel foods like corn.

3.) Necessary Procedures

In addition to feeding and housing your guinea fowl, there are a few other procedures you may need to perform. In this section you will learn the basics about wing clipping, culling, and preparing guinea fowl for the table.

a.) Wing Clipping

If you keep your guinea fowl penned rather than letting them roam free, you will need to clip their wings to keep them from escaping. Clipping your guinea fowl's wings will not be painful as long as you perform the procedure properly. Many guinea fowl owners choose to only clip the feathers on one wing – this keeps the guinea fowl from being able to achieve any height but still allows it to fly up to about 4 feet if they need to escape a predator or glide down from their roost.

Before clipping your guinea fowl's feathers, keep these key facts in mind:

- Only feathers that have fully grown in should be clipped – feathers that are still growing will have blood in the shaft

- Your guinea fowl will molt and regrow its feathers from time to time so you may need to re-clip the wings every few months

- If your guinea fowl are vulnerable to predator attacks, consider another method of containment rather than wing clipping which could leave the guinea fowl defenseless

- Use a pair of sharp scissors with rounded tips to clip your guinea fowl's wings

Now that you know the basics about clipping your guinea fowl's wings you are ready to learn the procedure. Below you will find a step-by-step guide for clipping your guinea fowl's wings:

1. Wrap your guinea fowl in a towel with one wing exposed – hold him tightly to keep him from breaking free.

2. Spread out the exposed wing to identify the primary flight feathers – look for the 10 long feathers on the outermost part of the bird's wing.

3. Check to make sure there is no blood in the shaft of the feathers.

4. Beginning with the feather furthest from the bird's body, clip one feather at a time – remove about ½ to $^2/_3$ of the feather's length.

5. Continue clipping the feathers one at a time until all ten have been cut.

b.) Culling

Even if you do not raise guinea fowl primarily for their meat, you may still be faced with the necessity of killing one or more members of your flock. While guinea fowl prefer to be kept in groups, there may be trouble if there are too many males in the group. Generally, one guinea cock can be counted on to fertilize up to 6 guinea hens on a regular basis – there is no reason to keep more guinea cocks than needed to meet this ratio.

If you have too many male guinea fowl in your flock, you may end up having problems. Not only will the guinea fowl be incredibly noisy, but they could also fight and injure each other. Because one guinea cock can be counted on to keep a harem of up to 6 guinea hens, there is no need to keep more males than necessary around. Culling may seem cruel but, in the end, it is the best way to keep the peace. After all, the next breeding season will yield new keets and you may not have room to keep all of them.

c.) Guinea Fowl for the Table

If you plan to sell your guinea fowl for food you will need to know the basics about the marketing season. Generally, the marketing season for poultry such as guinea fowl begins in late summer and carries throughout the fall. The highest demand is for young birds that weigh between 1.75 and 2.5 lbs. live, (about 1 kg). If you are raising the birds for your own use, the actual weight may not be as important.

Sometimes guinea fowl meat is referred to as the "poor man's pheasant" – it has a similar taste and texture to pheasant but it is much less expensive. Even if guinea fowl meat sells for half the cost of pheasant meat, it is still generally considered a delicacy. Guinea fowl meat is at home on the menus of upscale French and Oriental-style restaurants in cities all over the world.

Perhaps what makes guinea fowl meat such a delicacy is the fact that it is both richer and darker than chicken meat. Even so, guinea fowl meat is lower in both fat and calories than chicken meat. Though guinea fowl have large, rounded bodies, they are smaller-boned than chickens are and they have much larger, heavier breasts. The average broiler chicken dresses out to an average of 70% of its live weight but a guinea fowl dresses out to 75%.

One thing to consider in regard to eating guinea fowl is that the meat of guinea hens is preferable to the meat of a guinea cock. Young 12-week old keets, however, provide the most flavorful meat of all. The butchering and dressing process for guinea fowl is the same as for chicken and you should chill the meat quickly after butchering, covering it loosely for up to 2 days. To freeze guinea fowl meat you should package it securely with plastic wrap and place it in a plastic freezer bag. Guinea fowl meat will keep for up to six months when frozen.

In regard to preparation methods, cooking guinea fowl meat is very similar to cooking chicken – you can use guinea fowl in any recipe that calls for chicken. Young guinea fowl are best broiled, fried or roasted. Older guinea hens or cocks are best cooked by roasting at a temperature of 350°F (177°C) for about 45 minutes until it is tender and cooked through. One very popular method of preparing guinea hen is to wrap it in bacon before roasting.

Chapter Six: Breeding Guinea Fowl

Many people who keep guinea fowl also choose to breed their guinea fowl. Even if you do not actively attempt to breed your guinea fowl, they may breed on their own. Breeding guinea fowl is not difficult and it generally does not require any special equipment or housing. In this chapter you will learn the basics about guinea fowl breeding including preparation tips for guinea fowl hens and information about caring for guinea fowl eggs.

1.) Basic Breeding Info

Before you can attempt to breed your guinea fowl, you need to understand the basics about how they breed. In many cases, guinea fowl are monogamous which means that they select one mate for life. In some species, however, the male will mate with more than one female. When the pair are ready to breed you may notice some courtship behavior. The male will strut for the female, exhibiting a humped posture. If the female is receptive, the two will mate and the female will lay fertile eggs.

It is important to note that guinea fowl are seasonal breeders. During the winter, guinea fowl are likely to roam around in one large group but as spring approaches, the flock will break into smaller groups composed of four to six guinea fowl – one male, the rest female. Also during this time the male guinea fowl may start to challenge each other in order to establish supremacy. You may also notice the males starting to chase the females. It is unlikely that you will witness your guinea fowl actually mating, but you may see the male attempt to mount a female from time to time.

Once mating has occurred, the female will lay her eggs. The average clutch size for guinea fowl varies depending on the breed but, for the most part, the average clutch contains 6 to 12 eggs. Guinea fowl are ground-nesters so they will lay their eggs in the grass where they will then incubate them for the next 26 to 28 days. If you have free-ranging guinea fowl you may be able to identify a hen who is preparing to lay eggs with the following clues:

- The hen revisits a certain area of undergrowth often (she may be preparing a nest).
- The hen spends extended periods of time in that patch of undergrowth.
- The hen begins to dig a hole in the area to build a nest.
- Male guinea fowl begin to wait near the nest for the female to come by.

Female guinea fowl are capable of laying eggs once they reach the age of 16 weeks. Unless the hen reaches this age in the late winter or early spring, she will typically wait until the next breeding season to begin laying. If you happen upon a guinea fowl nest with more than the average number of eggs in it, it is likely that more than one hen is using the nest.

2.) The Breeding Process

If you allow your guinea fowl to be free-range, you may find it very difficult to locate their nests. Guinea fowl tend to hide their nests in patches of brambles or nettle. In order to find a guinea fowl nest, you will need to observe the behavior of the birds for several days during which you expect them to be laying. When the female lays her eggs, the male guinea fowl will typically stand guard against predators – when you see this type of behavior it is a good bet that you will find a nest nearby.

If you plan to collect the guinea fowl eggs – whether to eat them or hatch them out – you need to be careful how you approach the nest. Not only is it likely for guinea fowl to nest in stinging nettles, but you should be careful to disturb the nest as little as possible. If the nest is left in the condition you found it, there is a possibility that the guinea fowl will lay their next clutch of eggs in the nest. In most cases, however, the guinea fowl will move the nest for the next clutch and you will have to go on the hunt all over again the second time.

Once you have gathered the guinea fowl eggs, you need to decide whether you want to eat them or hatch them out. Guinea fowl eggs can be stored for up to 7 days before you absolutely need to start incubating them, so you have a little bit of time to make your decision. If you plan to hatch out the eggs you will need to use this time to prepare your incubator. Guinea fowl eggs require specific conditions in order to incubate properly so it is important that you do not rush the process of preparing your incubator.

3.) Raising the Babies

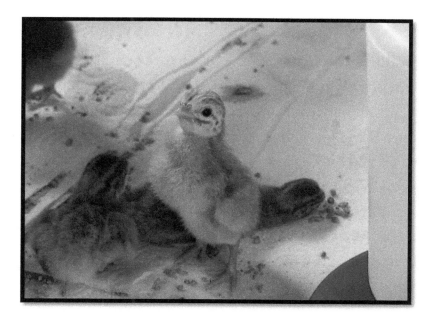

If you have decided that you want to hatch out your guinea fowl eggs, you will need to prepare an egg incubator for guinea fowl that keeps the eggs at the proper temperature. When you are storing the eggs before incubation, be sure to keep them at a temperature between 64.5° and 68°F (18° to 20°C). Once you place the eggs in the incubator, however, they will need to be kept at a temperature around 99.5°F (37.5°C). During the last 3 days of incubation you should drop the temperature to 98.5°F (36.5°C) to encourage hatching.

In addition to keeping your guinea fowl eggs at a certain temperature during incubation, you also need to maintain a specific humidity level. The ideal humidity for incubating guinea fowl eggs is about 65% for the first 25 days and then 80% during the last few days before hatching. The method by which you maintain this humidity level will vary depending on the type of incubator you have, but most models utilize water troughs to maintain humidity so you will need to check the troughs often and refill them as needed throughout the incubation period.

Another thing you need to do while your guinea fowl eggs are incubating is to rotate them daily – this also applies to the storage period before incubation. If you have an incubator that includes an automatic egg turner you should set it to turn the eggs every four hours. If you will be turning the eggs by hand, you need only turn them once daily. Plan to turn the guinea fowl eggs every day for the first 25 then let them rest for the final day or two before hatching. At this point you will also need to add more water to the troughs to raise the humidity to 80%.

About 24 hours before the eggs start to hatch, you will hear a pipping noise coming from the eggs. For the most part, all of the guinea fowl eggs should hatch within 28 days but weaker keets may take a day or two longer. Once the keets have hatched, leave them in the incubator until they are completely dry – if you take them out too soon they could catch a chill and die. When the keets are dry, transfer them to a brooder and give them fresh water and chick crumbs as soon as you transfer them. If any unhatched eggs remain four days after the main group has hatched you can safely assume that they are infertile or that the keet has died and you can discard the eggs. After removing the keets, be sure to thoroughly clean and disinfect the incubator.

Your guinea fowl brooder should be maintained at a temperature between 95° and 100°F (35° to 38°C) for the first two weeks. After that point you should lower the temperature by about 5°F (15°C) per week until the 6th week in the brooder. After the sixth week, you no longer need to heat the brooder and you can transfer the keets to a larger pen so they have room to grow. For the first six weeks, feed the keets commercial chick crumbs then switch to a commercial grower formula which will have a higher protein content to help the keets grow. Once the keets are about 16 to 20 weeks old you can feed them the same food you offer your adult guinea fowl.

Chapter Seven: Keeping Guinea Fowl Healthy

Guinea fowl are not terribly difficult to care for, but there are certain things you must do in order to keep your birds healthy. In addition to offering your guinea fowl a clean habitat and a healthy diet, you should familiarize yourself with common diseases so you can quickly diagnose and treat any problems that arise. In this chapter you will learn about some of the most common diseases to affect guinea fowl including their symptoms, cause, and treatment options. You will also receive tips for preventing disease.

1.) *Common Health Problems*

As long as you take care of your guinea fowl, you can expect them to reach a lifespan around 10 to 15 years. Unfortunately, guinea fowl are prone to developing certain diseases which can decrease their life expectancy. The best thing you can do for your guinea fowl is to familiarize yourself with common guinea fowl diseases so you can identify them quickly if they occur and seek the proper vet treatment. In this section you will learn about the diseases which commonly affect guinea fowl including the symptoms, causes, and treatment options.

Common guinea fowl diseases may include:

- Avian Encephalomyelitis
- Bacterial Infections
- Coccidiosis
- Infectious Coryza
- Lymphoid Leukosis
- Pullorum
- Ranikhet
- Roundworms
- Swollen Head Syndrome
- Turkey Rhinotracheitis

Avian Encephalomyelitis

This disease tends to infect young birds, most commonly within the first week after hatching though it can affect keets up to six weeks after hatching. Avian encephalomyelitis is caused by avian encephalomyelitis virus (AEV), a type of hepatovirus that is known to cause epidemic tremors in infected birds. Though most commonly found in chickens, this disease can also affect other poultry including guinea fowl.

AEV can be spread both horizontally or vertically through direct contact with an infected bird, from hen to keet (through the egg), or through fecal contamination of water or feed. Once a bird has recovered from the disease it is immune to further infection and cannot spread the disease. Common signs of this communicable disease include dullness of the eyes, loss of coordination, tremors of the neck and head, and eventually paralysis or prostration. Unfortunately, there is no treatment for this disease and it is recommended that infected birds be killed. Fortunately, there is a vaccine available against this disease.

Bacterial Infections

One of the most dangerous bacterial infections seen in guinea fowl is *E. coli* – the disease caused by this bacteria is referred to as colibacillosis. This disease is most common in young keets between 8 and 10 weeks of age, frequently due to damp flooring and poor hygiene practices. Sawdust is a very common type of litter used in brooders and guinea fowl pens. During wet weather and winter, the sawdust can become damp which makes it a perfect breeding ground for the *E. coli* bacteria. The most common method of transmission for this bacteria is through fecal contamination of feed, water, and litter.

Unfortunately, the symptoms of *E. coli* are easily confused for other diseases. For keets infected with *E. coli*, death usually occurs within three days of hatching. In adults, colibacillosis may present with some of the same symptoms as bird flu in guinea fowl. Treatment for this bacterial infection may include vaccination with a live *E. coli* vaccine, antibiotic treatments, and enhanced hygiene practices. The best way to prevent this disease is through vaccinating guinea fowl and keeping proper sanitary measures in place.

Coccidiosis

Coccidiosis in guinea fowl is the result of a protozoan parasite called coccidian. Guinea fowl may be exposed to this parasite through damp conditions, contaminated water or litter, and direct contact with infected birds. The parasite may be passed through the feces and spread to other birds in that manner as well. Infections due to intestinal parasites in guinea fowl such as coccidiosis may cause symptoms such as bloody diarrhea, paleness, weakness, and death. Other symptoms may include unthriftiness, increased thirst, and the head being drawn back to the shoulders.

Diagnosis of coccidiosis can be made through observation of parasite symptoms in guinea fowl as well as fecal tests. The first step in treating this disease is to isolate the infected birds and to medicate them through food and water. Prevention is the most effective treatment method, however, and it is also fairly easy. Feeding guinea fowl coccidiostats as they grow can help them to develop an immunity. You should also take basic sanitary precautions and avoid dampness in the litter.

Infectious Coryza

This disease is caused by the bacteria Haemophilus paragallinarum and it can be highly infectious. Infectious coryza is sometimes chronic in nature, but it is more commonly an acute infection. The main symptom associated with this disease is catarrhal inflammation of the upper respiratory tract – essentially, a lung infection in guinea fowl. Some signs of this disease include facial swelling, nasal discharge, sneezing, swollen wattle, loss of condition, and lack of appetite. Post-mortem tests will also reveal lesions in the respiratory tract.

Infectious coryza is typically transmitted through direct contact with infected birds, though it can also be spread through inhalation of airborne droplets or through contact with contaminated feed or water. Birds that recover from the disease remain carriers throughout the rest of their lives. Treatment options for this disease include medication with water-soluble antibiotics such as sulfadimethoxine, erythromycin, or tetracycline. Proper sanitation methods are the best form of prevention though vaccines are available for flocks that have been exposed to the disease.

Lymphoid Leukosis

This disease is caused by several viruses within the leukosis/sarcoma grouping of avian retroviruses – these viruses are typically divided into subgroups A, B, C, D, and J based on viral differences. Though chickens are the natural host for all of the viruses within the leukosis/sarcoma grouping, this disease can be spread to other poultry including guinea fowl. Unfortunately, this disease has a long incubation period (about 4 months), so the disease may be fairly advanced before the bird ever shows symptoms of disease.

Some of the most common symptoms of lymphoid leukosis in guinea fowl include weakness, weight loss, swelling of the abdomen, and greenish diarrhea. This disease can be transmitted through the egg from hen to keet or through direct contact within the flock. This virus is not spread by air, but it can be transmitted by contact with contaminated environments. There is no treatment for this disease but it can be prevented by eradicating carriers from breeding stock so it cannot be spread to keets.

Pullorum

Though turkeys and chicken are the types of poultry most susceptible to pullorum disease, all types of birds can potentially be infected. This disease is caused by a sub-species of Salmonella bacteria and, for this reason, it is sometimes referred to as Salmonella Pullorum or simply Pullorum Disease (PD). Pullorum disease can infect both adult guinea fowl and their keets. In keets, this disease causes the birds to be weak, having a poor appetite and stunted growth – infected keets typically die soon after hatching unless they are infected after hatching, in which case they die within two to three weeks.

In adult guinea fowl, pullorum disease can cause depression, diarrhea, dehydration and poor appetite. If the bird survives the disease, he may still have a poor growth rate and underdeveloped body. This disease is transmitted through direct contact with an infected bird, from hen to chick, or from fecal contamination of feed, water, or litter. Unfortunately, this disease cannot be treated – it is recommended that infected birds be culled to prevent the spread of the disease by even recovered birds.

Ranikhet

Also referred to as Newcastle disease, ranikhet disease (or simply ranikhet) is caused by avian paramyxovirus type 1 (APMV-1). This disease is incredibly contagious and lethal – it can even be transmitted to humans and other mammals. Ranikhet manifests in three different forms – mildly pathogenic (lentogenic), moderately pathogenic (mesogenic), or highly pathogenic (velogenic). Some of the symptoms of this disease include hoarse chirping in keets, a watery nasal discharge, labored breathing, swelling of the face, paralysis, trembling, or twisting of the neck.

Ranikhet can be transmitted very easily by inhalation or ingestion as well as through direct contact with contaminated birds, feed, water, or litter. Your veterinarian can diagnose this disease by observation of symptoms as well as the presence of lesions – lab tests can also be performed to identify the presence of antibodies. Unfortunately, no treatment has been found effective for ranikhet – infected birds should be quarantined for at least 15 days. There is a vaccine for this disease and good sanitation measures can help with prevention. This disease is not currently present in the United States.

Roundworms

Roundworms are a type of intestinal parasite in guinea fowl, commonly the parasite *Ascaridia galli*. These parasites are fairly large, measuring about 1.5 to 3 inches in length which makes them easily visible to the naked eye. This disease is commonly passed from hen to keet because it travels from the intestine of infected hens to the oviduct where it joins with the egg contents as the egg is being formed inside the hen. Some common symptoms of roundworm infection include emaciation, lethargy, and diarrhea – you may even see the parasite in expelled feces.

Unfortunately, available treatments kill only the adult parasite – any eggs that have been deposited inside the infected bird may still develop. Piperazine is the treatment of choice for this disease and it has a high rate of efficacy. Prevention methods are also important for the control of roundworms. Infected animals should be confined for treatment then the area should be thoroughly cleaned and disinfected to prevent re-infection.

Swollen Head Syndrome

Swollen head syndrome is caused by a pneumovirus belonging to the Paramyxoviridae family and it is common in several types of poultry including guinea fowl, chickens, turkey, and pheasants. This disease is easily transmitted through the air as well as by direct contact with infected birds and contaminated materials. Currently, swollen head syndrome is not present in the United States but it does occur in most other countries around the world.

Some of the most common symptoms of this disease include sneezing, reddening and swelling of tear ducts, facial swelling that extends over the head and down the jawline to the wattles, disorientation, twisting of the neck, and drop in egg production. Unfortunately, no medications have been proven effective in the treatment of this disease but antibiotics may be helpful in combating a portion of the disease. Prevention through vaccination is recommended, though live vaccines are not yet approved for use in the United States – only killed vaccines are recommended.

Turkey Rhinotracheitis

As suggested by the name, this disease most commonly affects turkeys but it can be transmitted to other types of poultry including guinea fowl. This disease affects birds of all ages, though it is typically most severe in keets. Turkey rhinotracheitis is caused by several viruses belonging to the pneumovirus genus called Paramyxoviridae. The morbidity rate for this disease is between 10% and 100% while the mortality rate is between 1% and 30%.

This disease can be transmitted laterally through direct contact with infected birds or with contaminated feed, water, or litter. Recovered birds remain carriers for the disease and can still transmit it to others. Some of the most common symptoms of this disease include hoarse chirps in keets, decreased appetite, sneezing, nasal discharge, drop in egg production, and de-pigmented or thin-shelled eggs. Unfortunately, antibiotic treatments are not very effective against this disease – there is also no usable vaccine available for this disease as of yet.

2.) Preventing Illness in Guinea Fowl

Though you may not be able to fully protect your guinea fowl from being exposed to certain diseases, there are many prevention methods you can employ. First, it is essential that you maintain proper sanitation practices to prevent the growth and spread of bacteria and parasites. Always thoroughly clean and disinfect your incubator and brooder between clutches and clean your feeders and water dishes on a regular basis. If you use litter or bedding in your coop or pen, change it often and make sure it does not become damp in wet weather or over the winter.

In addition to employing basic sanitation practices, you may also want to vaccinate your guinea fowl against certain diseases. Commercially-raised guinea fowl are commonly vaccinated due to the fact that large numbers of birds are kept in close quarters. If you have a small flock that doesn't come into contact with other poultry you may not need to vaccinate your guinea fowl. <u>In order to fully protect your guinea fowl, however, you may want to consider the following vaccinations</u>:

- Newcastle Disease (Ranikhet Disease)
- Avian Encephalomyelitis
- Infectious Coryza
- *E. coli* (live vaccine)
- Avian Rhinotracheitis

Again, it is up to you whether or not you choose to vaccinate your guinea fowl. If you take any of your birds to poultry shows, if you have had problems with a disease in the past, or if you plan to add new stock to your existing flock, however, you may want to consider it. Always consult your veterinarian before administering a vaccine and make sure you employ the proper route of administration per the specific vaccine.

Chapter Eight: Showing Guinea Fowl

Guinea fowl can be shown at most poultry shows and it can be an exciting challenge for the guinea fowl owner. Because there are specific standards for perfection in guinea fowl, however, you should not enter into the show arena lightly. Before you show your guinea fowl, take the time to familiarize yourself with the standards of perfection so you can be sure that your guinea fowl will do well. You will learn about the guinea fowl standard of perfection in this chapter.

1.) Standard of Perfection

Many guinea fowl breeders also choose to show their guinea fowl. Showing guinea fowl is an exciting challenge and it can be a great way to network with other breeders. Before you can show your guinea fowl, however, you need to familiarize yourself with the standards to which your bird will be compared. <u>Below you will find details regarding the standard of perfection for helmeted guinea fowl, the most popular species of guinea fowl for show</u>:

Size and Weight

When it comes to showing guinea fowl, there are specific standards for age and weight which help to divide the guinea fowl into different categories. The age and size classifications for guinea fowl are as follows:

- **Cock** – adult male, standard weight 4 lbs. (1.8 kg)
- **Cockerel** – male under 1 year, standard weight 3.5 lbs. (1.6 kg)
- **Hen** – adult female, standard weight 3.5 lbs. (1.6 kg)
- **Pullet** – female under 1 year, standard weight 3 lbs. (1.36 kg)

*Note: If the guinea fowl deviates from the standard weight by more than 20% (either up or down), it is an automatic disqualification. Deductions will be assessed as follows: 1 point deducted for each ¼ lbs. underweight; 1 point deducted for each ¼ lbs. overweight after the first ¼ lbs.

Male Shape and Appearance

The male guinea fowl should have a short, broad head with a triangular helmet that slopes slightly downward toward the rear. The face, head and neck are devoid of feathers with a narrow band of plumage starting at the base of the helmet and running down the back of the head – this band widens as it approaches and connects to the hackle.

The beak is short and stout, the eyes large and round with an alert expression. The wattles should be stiff and smooth, both of them cupped and carried at a 90-degree angle to the side of the head. The neck and hackle are covered with fine feathers, the tail short and carried low. The breast is prominent and well-rounded, the back broad and curving toward the tail. The wings are large and wide, carried horizontally. The shanks are short and un-feathered, with four toes on the feet without spurs.

Female Shape and Appearance

The female's shape and appearance is the same as the male except for the helmet being smaller and narrower. The wattle may be either tucked or cupped. In terms of carriage, the female should be upright, though the stance may be less upright than the male's.

Standards for Colored Guinea Fowl

Colored guinea fowl may be pearl, lavender, or white. For the pearl color, plumage is blue-grey throughout the body, generously dotted with white pearl-like spots or wavy bars of white. The beak should be reddish-horn, the eyes dark brown or black, and the helmet light brown in adult birds. The primary feathers are light blue-gray with parallel wavy bars of white on the inner rows and pearl-like dots on the outer rows.

Lavender guinea fowl exhibit the same patterning as the pearl variant but with the ground color of the plumage being a light gray or lavender. The shanks and toes of the bird are light gray or orange. Any indistinct pearls or barring on the wings is considered a defect.

White guinea fowl should have pure white plumage in all sections for both males and females. Though black feathers are allowed on the lower neck and hackle, they are not preferred. Both yellow cast and black flecking are considered a serious defect, as are spotty shanks or toes. The eyes should be light bay to brown in color.

Breakdown of Points

The following scale of points is used to evaluate guinea fowl in comparison to the standard of perfection. Some aspects of the scale are divided between type and color.

Category	Type	Color	Total Points
Symmetry/Carriage	5	-	5
Condition	10	-	10
Weight	5	-	5
Head	4	1	5
Eyes	4	1	5
Helmet and Wattles	7	3	10
Neck	3	2	5
Back	8	4	1
Tail	4	3	7
Wings	6	3	9
Breast	8	3	11
Body and Fluff	6	2	8
Legs and Toes	5	3	8
Total	75	25	100

2.) *What to Know Before Showing*

In addition to knowing what standards your guinea fowl must meet in show, you should also know about the characteristics which might cause you to lose points or to have your guinea fowl disqualified entirely. If your guinea fowl exhibits any of these characteristics you may want to reconsider showing him because he may not do well.

On the following page you will find a list of defects and disqualifications for helmeted guinea fowl:

Defects in Guinea Fowl

- Mismatched wattle in birds of either sex – one tucked and one cupped (tucked wattle is carried laterally and flat, close to side of throat; cupped is concave and carried at a 90-degree angle to side of head)
- White feather(s) in any part of plumage for colored guinea fowl
- Colored feather(s) in any part of plumage for white guinea fowl
- Yellow hue or black flecking in the plumage of white guinea fowl

Disqualifications for Guinea Fowl

- One or more white primary or secondary feathers in a colored guinea fowl
- One or more colored primary or secondary feathers in a white guinea fowl
- Mismatched wattles on young guinea fowl of either sex – one tucked and one cupped (tucked wattle is carried laterally and flat, close to side of throat; cupped is concave and carried at a 90-degree angle to side of head)

Chapter Nine: Guinea Fowl Care Sheet

In reading this book you have received a wealth of information about guinea fowls including their care, keeping, breeding, and feeding. In caring for your own guinea fowl, however, you may find that you have questions. Rather than flipping through the entire book to find the answer to your question, in this chapter you will find a care sheet of the most important guinea fowl information including tips for housing, feeding, and breeding your guinea fowl.

1.) Basic Information

Taxonomy: order Galliformes, subfamily Numididae

Number of Species: six main species, several subspecies and color variants

Habitat: sub-Saharan Africa, some more localized to certain areas or habitats

Domestication: helmeted guinea fowl most popular domesticated species

Purposes: pest control (insects), food source for humans, security against birds of prey, pets

Appearance: large, ground-nesting fowl; larger and heavier than chickens

Plumage: black or dark grey, densely covered with small white spots

Color Variants: pearl, slate, purple, chocolate, lavender, coral blue, pewter, bronze, blonde, and pied

Sexing: males tend to have larger helmets and wattles at maturity; males make one-note call, females two-note call

Size: 21 to 23 inches (53 to 58cm) tall

Weight: about 2.8 lbs. (1.3 kg)

2.) Habitat Guidelines

Housing Options: enclosed pen/coop; free-range during the day and cooped at night; completely free-range

Free-Range Disadvantages: guinea fowl will be wild; increased risk for predation; egg-laying will occur in the grass; keets may not survive if left to fend for themselves

Shelter for Free-Range: three-sided shelter, old barn, shed; ideally, south-facing

Penning: provide at least 30 square feet per dozen birds; cover with chicken netting or pinion birds

Coop Training: keep birds in pen/coop for 6 to 8 weeks then allow them to roam freely during the day

Coop Size: 3 square feet per bird plus 7 inches of roosting space each

3.) Nutritional Information

Type of Diet: omnivorous

Free-Range Diet: insects, weeds, grass, seeds

Types of Insects: grasshoppers, flies, slugs, worms, caterpillars, ticks, beetles, mosquitoes and more

Other Nutritional Needs: greens are also necessary for healthy digestion; guinea fowl will eat grass, weeds, and dandelion greens

Penned Diet: commercial poultry diet; laying formula is recommended if regular diet won't meet protein needs

Protein Needs: 16% for adults

Protein Needs (keets): 24% to 26% for first few weeks; 18% to 20% for 5 to 8 weeks

Occasional Treats: alfalfa greens, sorghum, millet, wheat

Do Not Feed: corn, medicated feed, large-kernel foods

4.) Breeding Information

Breeding Type: monogamous; in some species, the male will mate with more than one female

Nesting Type: ground-nesting

Courtship Behavior: male may chase the female or strut for her with a humped-back posture

Nesting Behavior: hen selects a patch of undergrowth then digs a hole to prepare the nest; male guards the female as she lays the eggs

Breeding Season: Spring

Egg-Laying Age: 16 weeks or older

Average Clutch Size: 6 to 12 eggs; varies by species

Incubation Period: 26 to 28 days

Storage: eggs may be stored for up to 7 days before incubation is necessary

Storage Temperature: between 64.5° and 68°F (18° to 20°C)

Incubation Temperature: 99.5°F (37.5°C) for 25 days; drop to 98.5°F (36.5°C) for last 3 days

Incubation Humidity: 65% for the first 25 days and then 80% during the last few days

Egg Turning: daily if done by hand; every 4 hours if by automatic egg turner; stop turning after day 25

Signs of Hatching: pipping sound within 24 hours of hatching

Post-Hatching Care: allow keets to dry then transfer to brooder with water and chick crumbs; discard unhatched eggs after 4 days

Brooding Temperature: between 95° and 100°F (35° to 38°C) for 2 weeks; decrease temperature by 5°F (15°C) per week until week 6; discontinue heat after week 6

Feeding Keets: offer commercial chick crumbs for first 6 weeks

Raising Keets: transfer keets to a pen/run after week 6 and switch to commercial grower formula until week 20

Chapter Ten: Relevant Websites

Throughout this book you have received a wealth of information on the care and keeping of guinea fowl. Even after finishing this book, however, you may still have questions and you may need helping finding the materials you need to raise your own guinea fowl. In this chapter you will find a collection of relevant websites and additional resources for feeding guinea fowl, guinea fowl cages, and general information on guinea fowl.

1.) Food for Guinea Fowl

United States Websites:

"Poultry Feeders and Waterers." eFowl.com. <http://www.efowl.com/Poultry_Feeders_and_Waterers_s/2 98.htm>

"Feeding Guinea Fowl: How to Feed Guineas for Optimum Poultry Health." Raising-Guineas.com. <http://raising-guineas.com/feedingguinea.html>

"Guinea Fowl Diet." GuineaFowl.com. <http://www.guineafowl.com/fritsfarm/guineas/diet/>

"Chicken Feed." Purina Mills. <http://purinamills.com/chicken-feed/>

"Nutrena Poultry Feeds." Nutrena.com. <www.nutrenaworld.com/products/poultry/>

United Kingdom Websites:

"Feeding." Guinea Fowl UK. <http://www.guinea-fowl.co.uk/05-feeding.html>

"Farmgate Poultry Food." Farmgate Feeds. <http://www.farmgatefeeds.co.uk/Poultry>

"Chicken Food and Grit." Green Valley Poultry Supplies. <http://www.chicken-house.co.uk/acatalog/Poultry_Feed___Grit.html>

"Chicken and Poultry." Pet-Supermarket.co.uk. <http://www.pet-supermarket.co.uk/Category/Caged_Bird_Supplies-Chicken_Poultry?ResultsPerPage=36>

2.) Cages for Guinea Fowl

United States Websites:

"Coop Building Supplies." eFowl.com.
<http://www.efowl.com/Chicken_Wire_Netting_and_Fenci
ng_Supplies_s/303.htm>

"Guinea Fowl Housing Ideas." GuineaFowl.com.
<http://www.guineafowl.com/fritsfarm/guineas/housing/>

Gibson, Cindy. "Training Your Guineas to Go Into the Coop
at Night." Guinea Fowl International.
<http://guineafowl.international/articles/training.php>

"Guinea Fowl and Housing Plans." Razor Family Farms.
<http://razorfamilyfarms.com/animals/guinea-fowl/guinea-
fowl-housing-plans/>

United Kingdom Websites:

"Chicken Coops." Flyte So Fancy.
<http://www.flytesofancy.co.uk/chickenhouses/Chicken_Co
ops.html>

Preston, Erica. "How to Build a Guinea Fowl House."
eHow.co.uk. <http://www.ehow.co.uk/how_6925022_build-
guinea-fowl-house.html>

"Country Chicken Coop." Buttercup Farm.
<http://www.buttercupfarm.co.uk/country-chicken-
coop.html>

"Chicken Houses, Poultry Supplies, and Complete
Packages." Chicken House Company.
<http://www.thechickenhousecompany.co.uk/>

3.) General Info for Guinea Fowl

United States Websites:

"Raising Guinea Fowl." University of Kentucky College of Agriculture, Food and Environment. <http://www2.ca.uky.edu/agc/pubs/ASC/ASC209/ASC209.pdf>

"Guinea Fowl: Color Chart for Adults and Keets." GuineaFowl.com. <http://www.guineafowl.com/fritsfarm/guineas/colors/>

"Guinea Fowl Breeds." Raising-Guineas.com. <http://raising-guineas.com/guineabreeds.html>

"Raising Guinea Fowl on the Homestead." Mother Earth News. <http://www.motherearthnews.com/homesteading-and-livestock/raising-guinea-fowl-zmaz03onzgoe.aspx#axzz3Ih8OmiJi>

United Kingdom Websites:

Guinea Fowl UK. <http://www.guinea-fowl.co.uk/ index.html>

Patton, Ellen R. and Jeannette S. Ferguson. "Gardening with Guineas: A Step-by-Step Guide to Raising Guinea Fowl." <http://www.amazon.co.uk/Gardening-Guineas-Step-By-Step-Raising-Guinea/dp/0739202502>

"Guinea Fowl." Small Holder Range. <http://www.smallholderfeed.co.uk/articles/breed-in-focus/Guinea-fowl.aspx>

"Articles and Activities." Guinea Fowl International. <http://guineafowl.international/articles/>

Index

A

B

C

D

E

F

K

L

M

N

neck	18, 19, 22, 68, 74, 76, 82, 84
needs	7, 43, 48, 49, 91
nest	34, 59, 60, 61, 92
Newcastle Disease	79
noise	24, 25, 30, 64
nose	3, 41
Numida	8, 14, 15, 114
Numididae	8, 12, 89
nutritional needs	48

O

origins	13

P

paralysis	68, 74
parasite	70, 75
patterns	1, 11, 16
pen	45, 46, 64, 78, 90, 93
perch	6
permit	27
pests	2, 23, 33
pets	3, 2, 5, 7, 8, 12, 23, 25, 33, 89
pheasants	1, 76
Pinioning	45
plumage	1, 10, 11, 15, 16, 18, 20, 22, 82, 83, 84, 87
plumed guinea fowl	9, 18, 19
Plumed Guinea Fowl	14, 18
pneumovirus	76, 77

| wing clipping | 42, 51, 52 |
| wings | 4, 22, 47, 51, 52, 82, 84, 114 |

Y

| yolk | 6 |

Z

| zoning restrictions | 27, 28, 34 |

Photo Credits

Cover Page Photo By Jamain via Wikimedia Commons,
<http://upload.wikimedia.org/wikipedia/commons/thumb/7
/78/Guinea_fowl_J2.jpg/1280px-Guinea_fowl_J2.jpg>

Page 1 Photo By Steve via Wikimedia Commons,
<http://upload.wikimedia.org/wikipedia/commons/thumb/7
/70/Helmeted_guinea_fowl.jpg/1024px-
Helmeted_guinea_fowl.jpg>

Page 7 Photo By Gavindux via Wikimedia Commons,
<http://commons.wikimedia.org/wiki/File:Adult_Guinea_F
owl_Head.JPG>

Page 9 Photo By Jamain via Wikimedia Commons,
<http://commons.wikimedia.org/wiki/File:Guinea_fowl_J4.j
pg>

Page 15 Photo By Gouldingken via Wikimedia Commons,
<http://en.wikipedia.org/wiki/Helmeted_guineafowl#media
viewer/File:DSC_0905.JPG>

Page 16 Photo By Daniel Giraud Elliot via WIkimedia Commons, <http://en.wikipedia.org/wiki/White-breasted_guineafowl#mediaviewer/File:Agelastes_meleagrides.jpg>

Page 17 Photo By Daniel Giraud Elliot via Wikimedia Commons, <http://en.wikipedia.org/wiki/Black_guineafowl#mediaviewer/File:Agelastes_niger.jpg>

Page 19 Photo By Daniel Giraud Elliot via Wikimedia Commons, <http://en.wikipedia.org/wiki/Plumed_guineafowl#mediaviewer/File:Guttera_plumifera.jpg>

Page 20 Photo By Arabuko Sokoke N.P. via Wikimedia Commons, <http://en.wikipedia.org/wiki/Crested_guineafowl#mediaviewer/File:Flickr_-_Rainbirder_-_Crested_Guineafowl_(Guttera_pucherani_pucherani).jpg>

Page 21 Photo By Sankara Subramanian via Wikimedia Commons, <http://lv.wikipedia.org/wiki/P%C4%93r%C4%

BCvistu_dzimta#mediaviewer/File:Vulturine_Guineafowl_f
lapping_its_wings.jpg>

Page 25 Photo By Cyclonebill via Wikimedia Commons,
<http://commons.wikimedia.org/wiki/File:Spinat,_fettucine,
_auberginecreme_og_perleh%C3%B8nebryst_farseret_med
_gorgonzola_og_valn%C3%B8dder_(5597967635).jpg>

Page 26 Photo By Trish Steel via Wikimedia Commons,
<http://commons.wikimedia.org/wiki/File:Guinea_Fowl_-
geograph.org.uk-_505518.jpg>

Page 31 Photo By Trish Steel via Wikimedia Commons,
<http://commons.wikimedia.org/wiki/File:Peacock_and_Gu
inea_Fowl_-_geograph.org.uk_-_522550.jpg>

Page 35 Photo By Jamain via Wikimedia Commons,
<http://commons.wikimedia.org/wiki/File:Guinea_fowl_J6.j
pg>

Page 39 Photo By Keithimus via Wikimedia Commons, <http://commons.wikimedia.org/wiki/File:AbileneGuineaFowl2.JPG>

Page 42 Photo By Raghavan2010 via Wikimedia Commons, <http://commons.wikimedia.org/wiki/File:Nature_in_my_Backyard_Guinea_Fowl_Mylasandra_Raghavan_N.jpg>

Page 48 Photo By Calistemon via Wikimedia Commons, <http://commons.wikimedia.org/wiki/File:Guinea_fowl_keets_and_bantam_chicks.jpg>

Page 57 Photo By Calistemon via Wikimedia Commons, <http://upload.wikimedia.org/wikipedia/commons/thumb/0/0f/Guinea_fowl_keet_3.jpg/1280px-Guinea_fowl_keet_3.jpg>

Page 60 Photo By Calistemon via Wikimedia Commons, <http://upload.wikimedia.org/wikipedia/commons/thumb/1/14/Guinea_fowl_keet_1.jpg/1280px-Guinea_fowl_keet_1.jpg>

Page 62 Photo By Peepe via Wikimedia Commons, <http://en.wikipedia.org/wiki/File:Lavender_Keet.jpg>

Page 66 Photo By Notjake13 via Wikimedia Commons, <http://upload.wikimedia.org/wikipedia/commons/thumb/e /e3/Guinea_fowl_eye.jpg/1280px-Guinea_fowl_eye.jpg>

Page 78 Photo By Derek Harper via Wikimedia Commons, <http://commons.wikimedia.org/wiki/File:Guinea_fowl,_So uth_Whilborough_-_geograph.org.uk_-_1514945.jpg>

Page 80 Photo By Jamain via Wikimedia Commons, <http://commons.wikimedia.org/wiki/File:Guinea_fowl_J3.j pg>

Page 83 Photo By Peepe via Wikimedia Commons, <http://en.wikipedia.org/wiki/File:Adolescent_Lavender_G uineafowl.jpg>

Page 86 Photo By Fir0002 via Wikimedia Commons, <http://commons.wikimedia.org/wiki/File:Guinea_fowl.jpg>

Page 88 Photo By Elwood via Wikimedia Commons, <http://commons.wikimedia.org/wiki/File:Guinea_Fowl_On _Patrol_New_Elwood_H.L.S._-_geograph.org.uk_- _1747294.jpg>

Page 94 Photo By Jonathan Billinger via Wikimedia Commons, <http://commons.wikimedia.org/wiki/ File:Three_guinea_fowl_out_for_a_stroll_- _geograph.org.uk_-_500377.jpg>

References

"5 Reasons Not to Own Guinea Fowl." The Free Range Life. < http://thefreerangelife.com/5-reasons-not-to-own-guinea-fowl/>

"Captive Wildlife Licenses and Permits." Florida Fish and Wildlife Conservation Commission. <http://myfwc.com/license/captive-wildlife/>

"Choosing Healthy Chickens." Keeping-Chickens.me.uk. <http://keeping-chickens.me.uk/chickens/choosing-healthy-chickens>

"Coccidiosis of Poultry." University of Illinois College of Agriculture. <https://www.ideals.illinois.edu/bitstream/handle/2142/33299/1093041.pdf?sequence=2>

"Fancy Poultry 101: Learn the Basics of Showing Poultry." Poultry Show Central. <http://www.poultryshowcentral.com/Fancy_101.html>

Gilbert, Rebecca Randall. "Guinea Fowl for Tick Control." Feathersite.com. <http://www.feathersite.com/Poultry/Guineas/SPPAGuineaFowlForTickControl.html>

"Glossary of Poultry Terms." eFowl.com. <http://www.efowl.com/articles.asp?id=246>

"Glossary of Poultry Terms." University of Kentucky College of Agriculture, Food and Environment. <http://afspoultry.ca.uky.edu/extension-glossary>

"Guinea Fowl Breeding Behavior." Farming Friends. <http://farmingfriends.com/guinea-fowl-breeding-behaviour/>

"How Many Guinea Fowl Should I Obtain?" Backyard Chickens. <http://www.backyardchickens.com/t/689577/how-many-guinea-fowl-should-i-obtain>

"How to Clip Guinea Fowl Wings." Guinea Fowl International. <http://guineafowl.international/clipwings.pdf>

"Incubating Guinea Fowl Eggs." Farming Friends. <http://farmingfriends.com/incubating-guinea-fowl-eggs/>

"Infectious Coryza." The Poultry Site. <http://www.thepoultrysite.com/diseaseinfo/82/infectious-coryza>

"Keeping Guinea Fowl with Chickens." Poultry Keeper Forum. <http://poultrykeeperforum.com/viewtopic.php?f=6&t=8032>

"Overview of Avian Enchephalomyelitis." The Merck Veterinary Manual. <http://www.merckmanuals.com/vet/poultry/avian_encephalomyelitis/overview_of_avian_encephalomyelitis.html>

"Poultry Farms: General Regulations." Gov.uk. <https://www.gov.uk/poultry-farms-general-regulations>

"Poultry Production in MIssissippi - Parasitic Diseases (Internal)." Mississippi State University. <http://msucares.com/poultry/diseases/disparas.htm>

Prabu, M.J. "Diseases of Guinea Fowl and Their Management." The Hindu. <http://www.thehindu.com/seta/2005/11/17/stories/2005111700131600.htm>

"Pullorum Disease and Fowl Typhoid." University of New Hampshire Cooperative Extension. <http://extension.unh.edu/resources/files/Resource000793_Rep817.pdf>

"Raising Guinea Fowl." University of Kentucky College of Agriculture, Food and Environment. <http://www2.ca.uky.edu/agc/pubs/ASC/ASC209/ASC209.pdf>

"Raising Guinea Fowl 101." Backyard Chickens. <http://www.backyardchickens.com/t/312682/raising-guinea-fowl-101>

"Raising Guinea Fowl: A Low-Maintenance Flock." Mother Earth News. <http://www.motherearthnews.com/homesteading-and-livestock/raising-guinea-fowl-zmaz92aszshe.aspx?PageId=6#axzz3Ih8OmiJi>

"Ranikhet Disease." Regional Disease Diagnostic Laboratory. <https://ahd.maharashtra.gov.in/pdf/dis/Ranikhet%20Disease.pdf>

"Sexing Guinea Fowl." GuineaFowl.com. <http://www.guineafowl.com/fritsfarm/guineas/sexing/>

"Standard of Perfection – Helmeted Guinea Fowl." GuineaFowl.com. <http://www.guineafowl.com/standards.html>

"Starting with Keets – How to Raise Guinea Fowl Keets." Guinea Fowl International. <http://guineafowl.international/articles/keets.php>

"The Guinea Fowl." Big Run Wolf Ranch. <http://www.bigrunwolfranch.org/guinea_fowl.html>

"Vaccination of Small Poultry Flocks." University of Florida Cooperative Extension Service. <http://mysrf.org/pdf/pdf_poultry/p8.pdf>

"When do Female Guinea Fowl Start Laying." Farming Friends. <http://farmingfriends.com/when-do-female-guinea-fowl-start-laying/>

"Wild Birds and the Law." Nature Net. <http://naturenet.net/law/birds.html>

CPSIA information can be obtained
at www.ICGtesting.com
Printed in the USA
BVHW01s0130030418
512330BV00004B/8/P